Coloring Book

Carlos Barahona

ISBN-13: 978-1523355617

ISBN-10: 1523355611

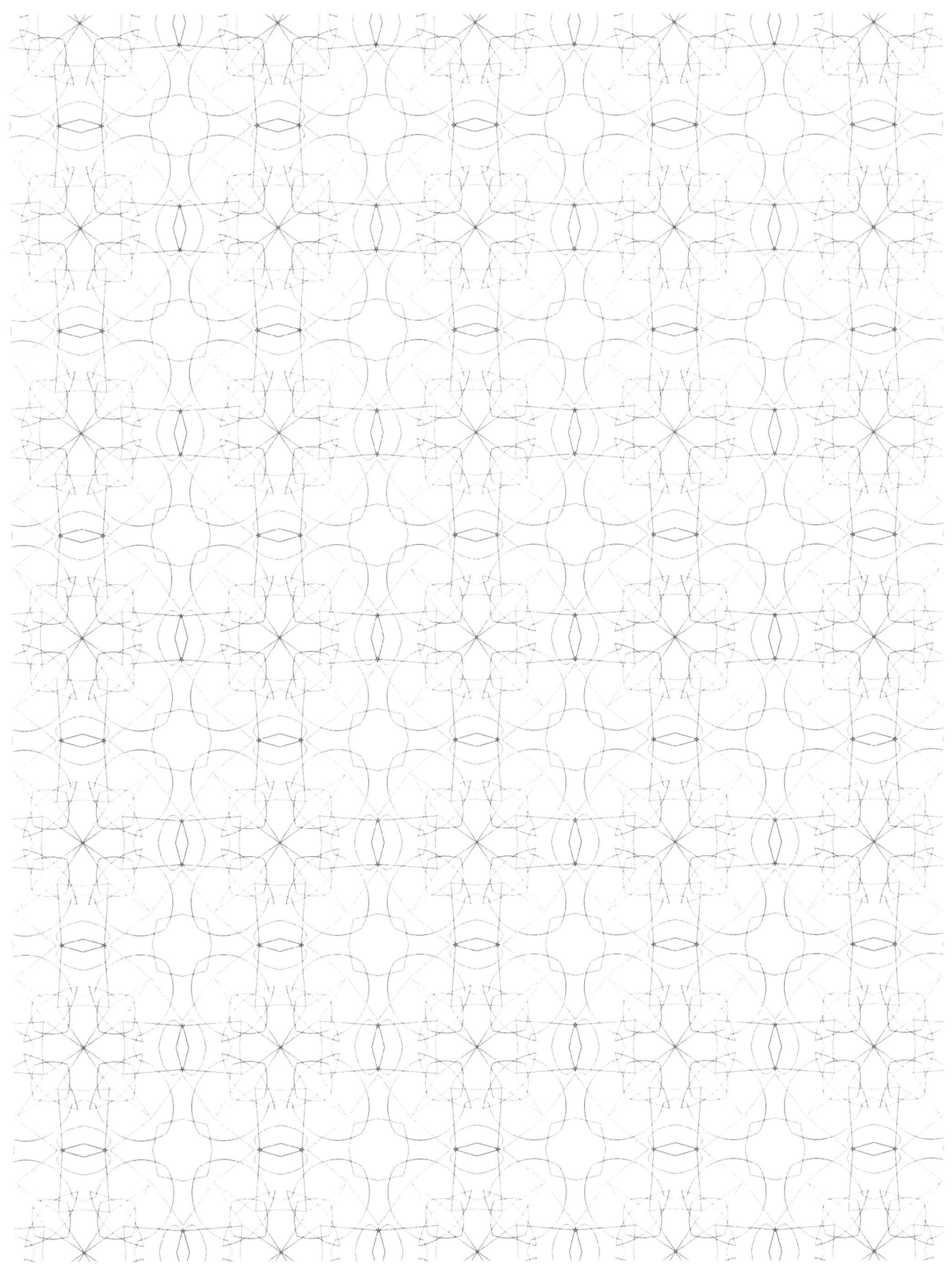

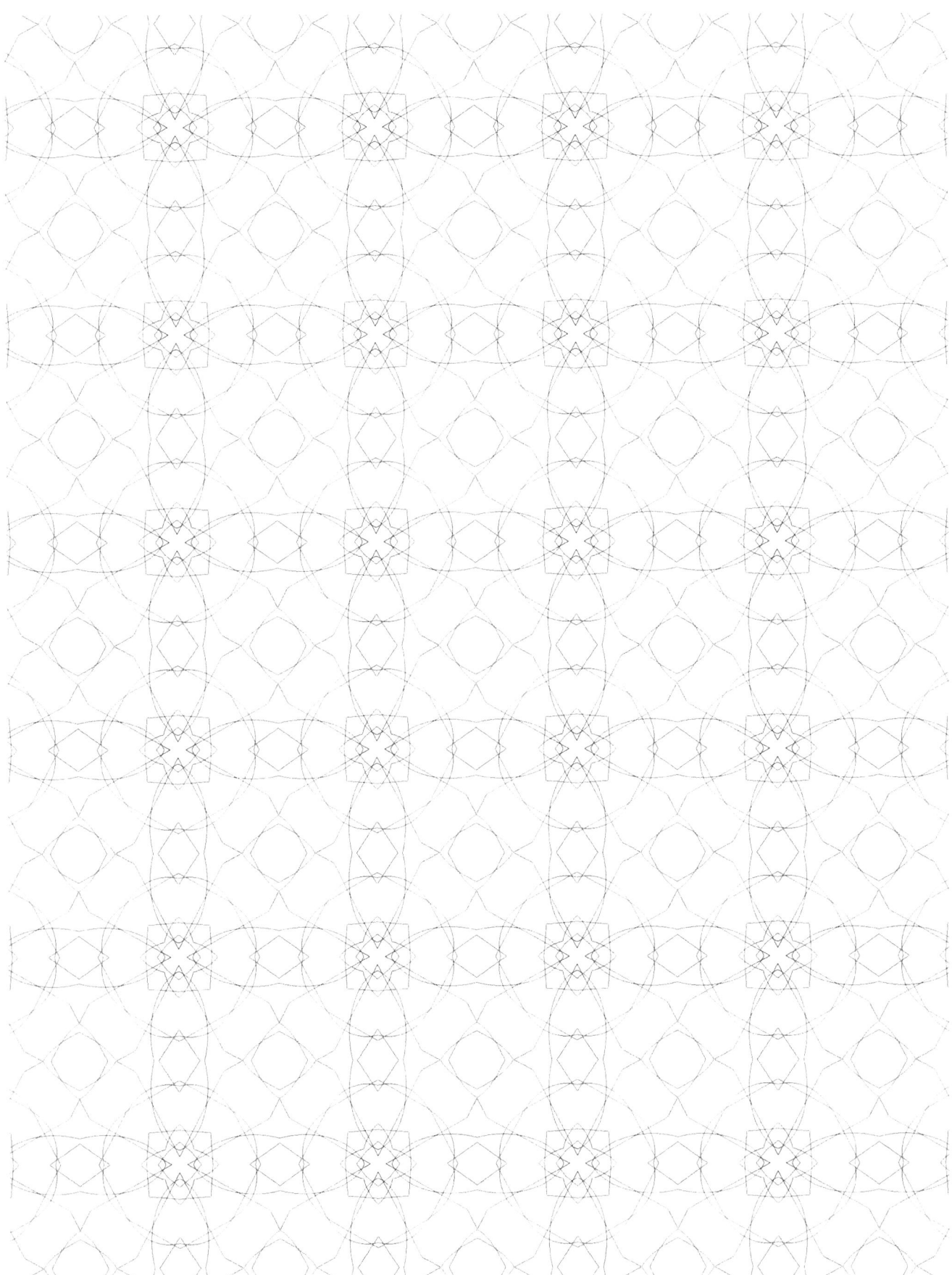

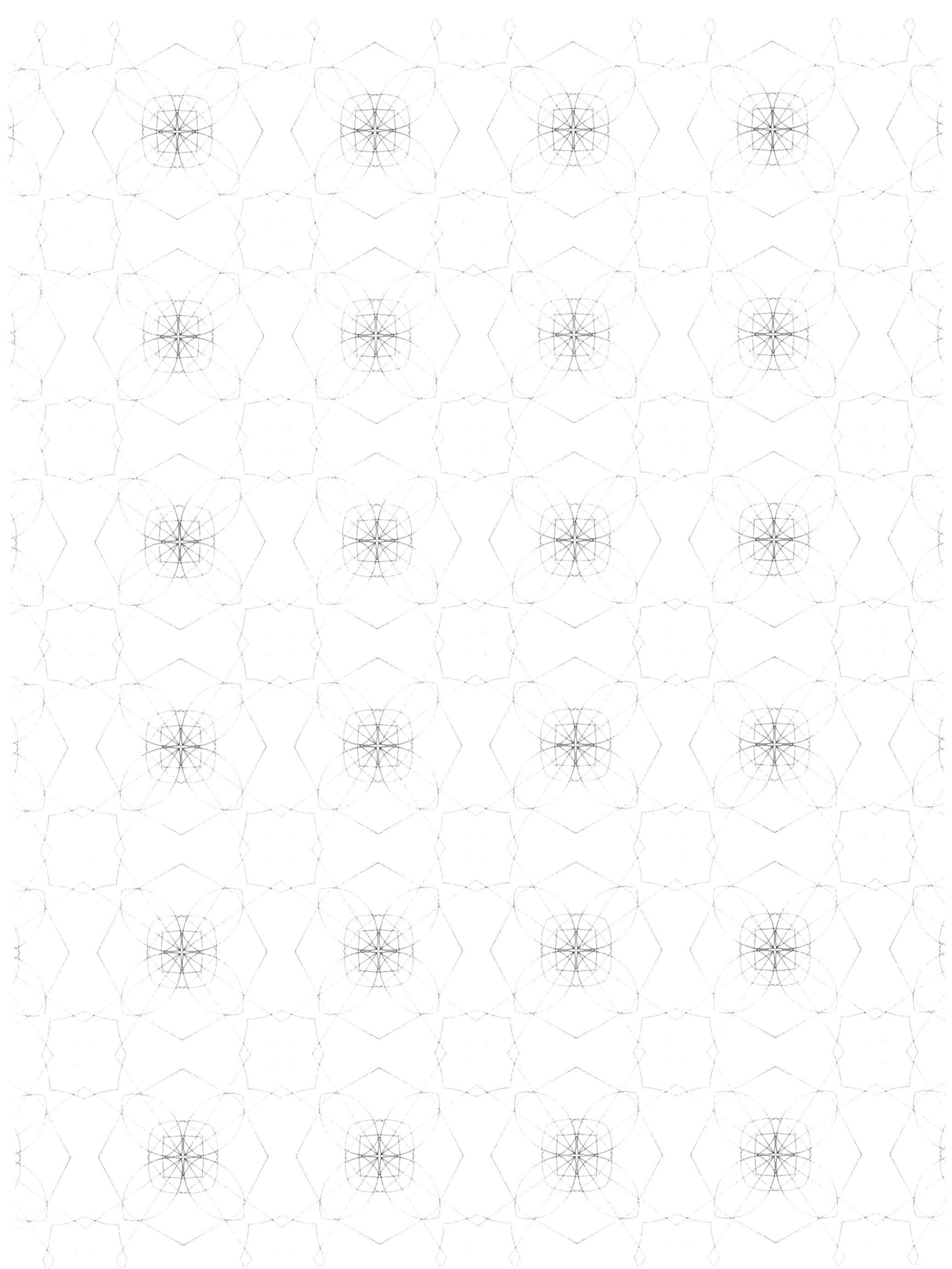

16

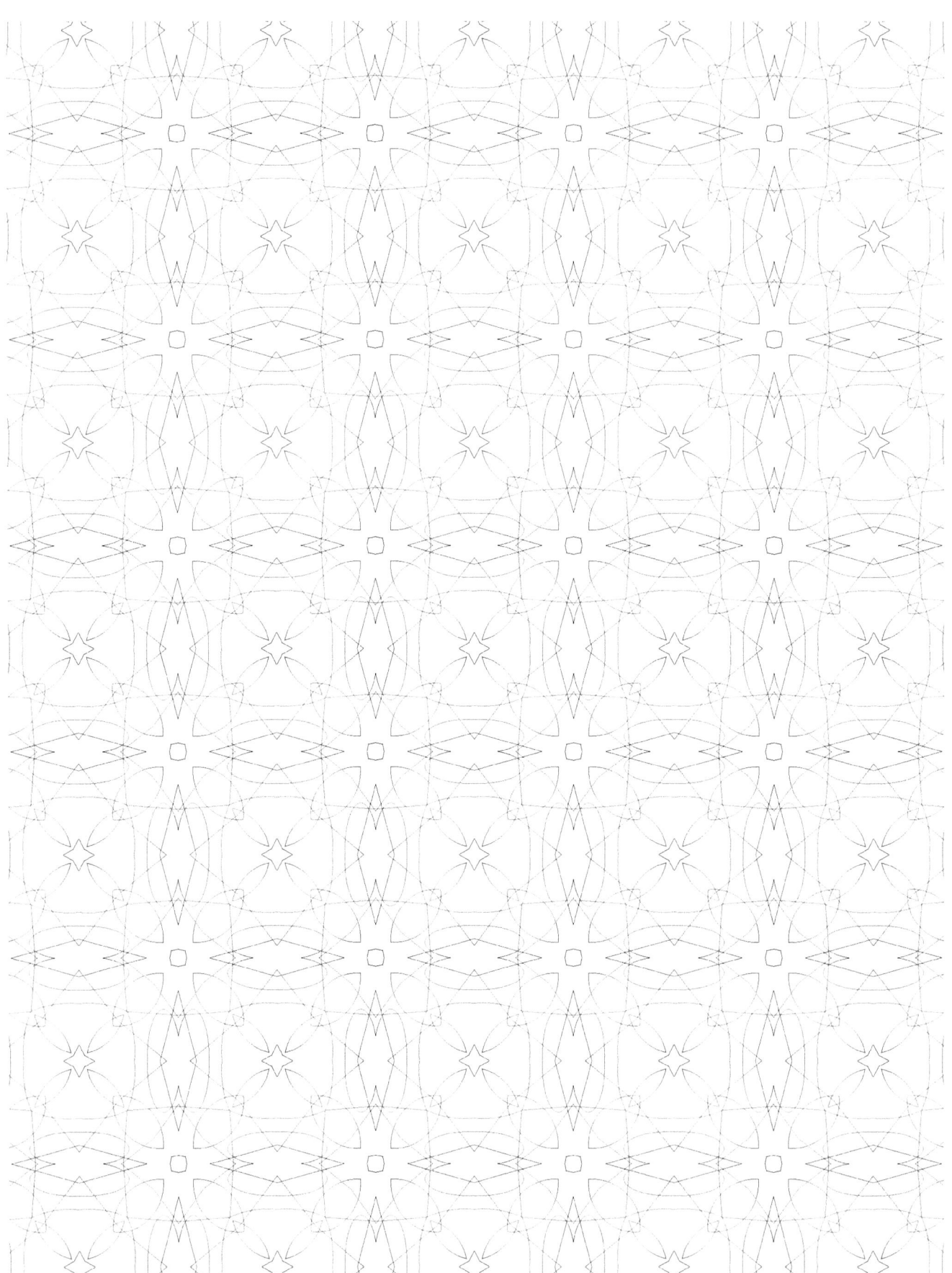

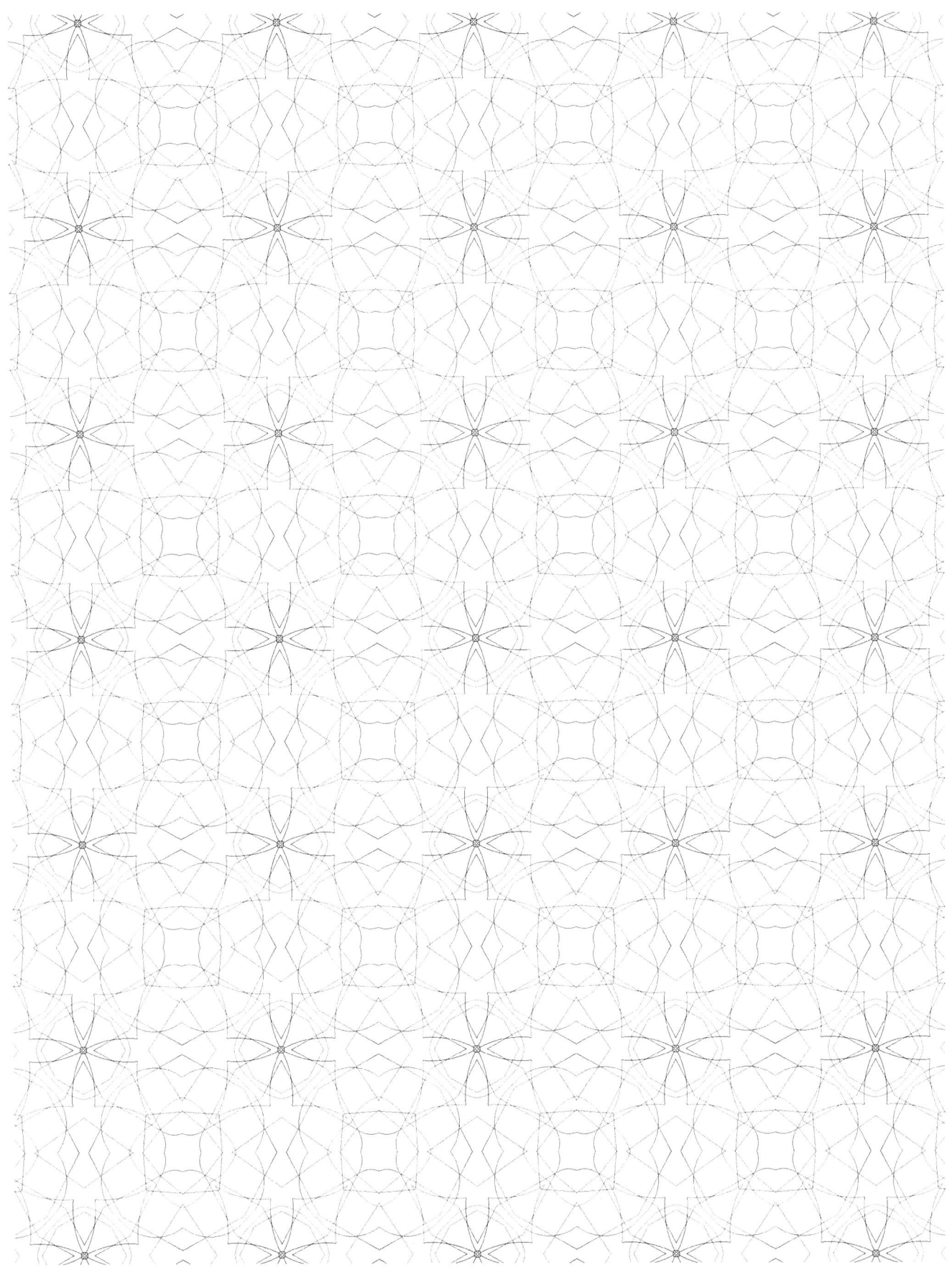

21

23

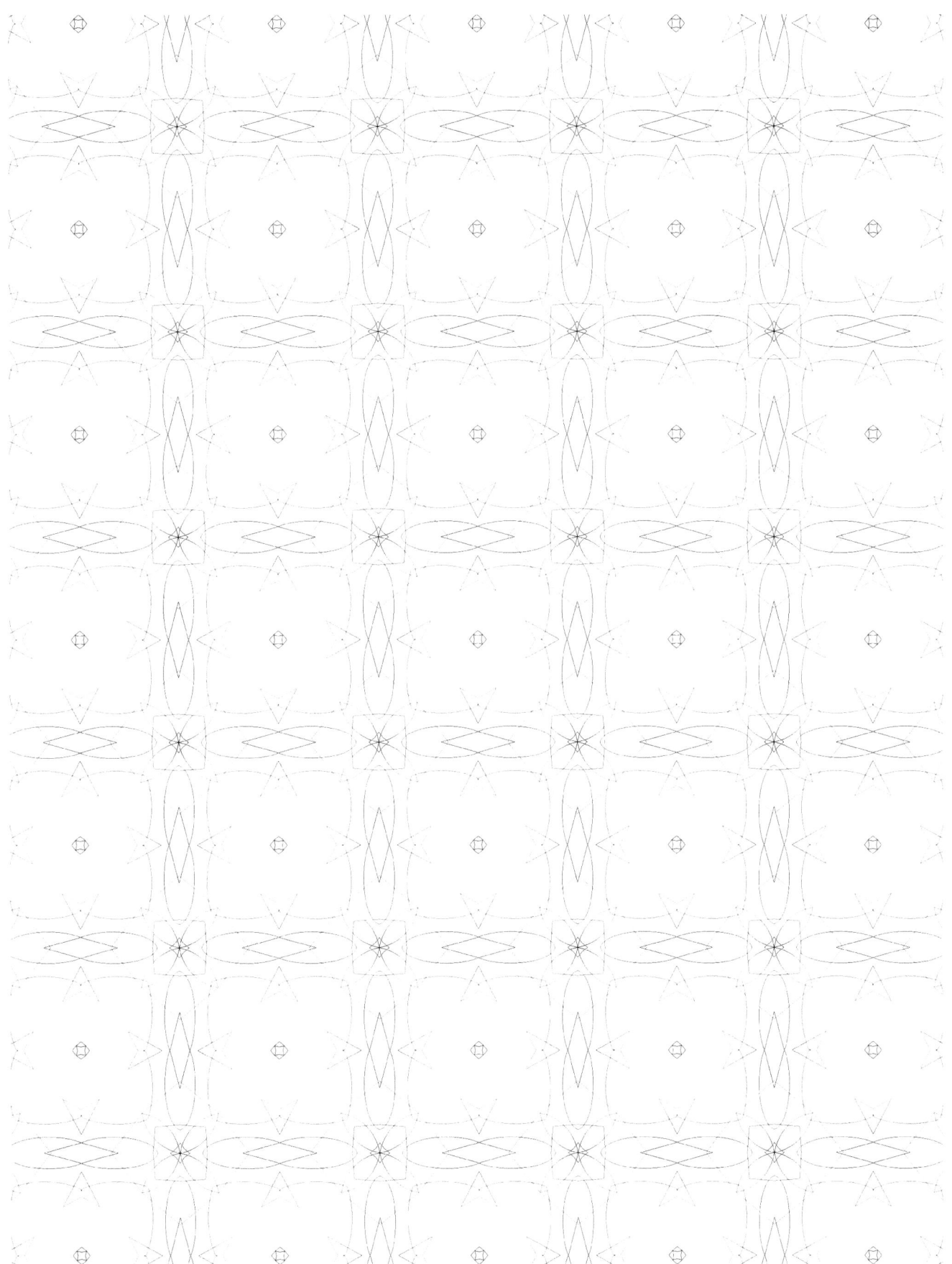

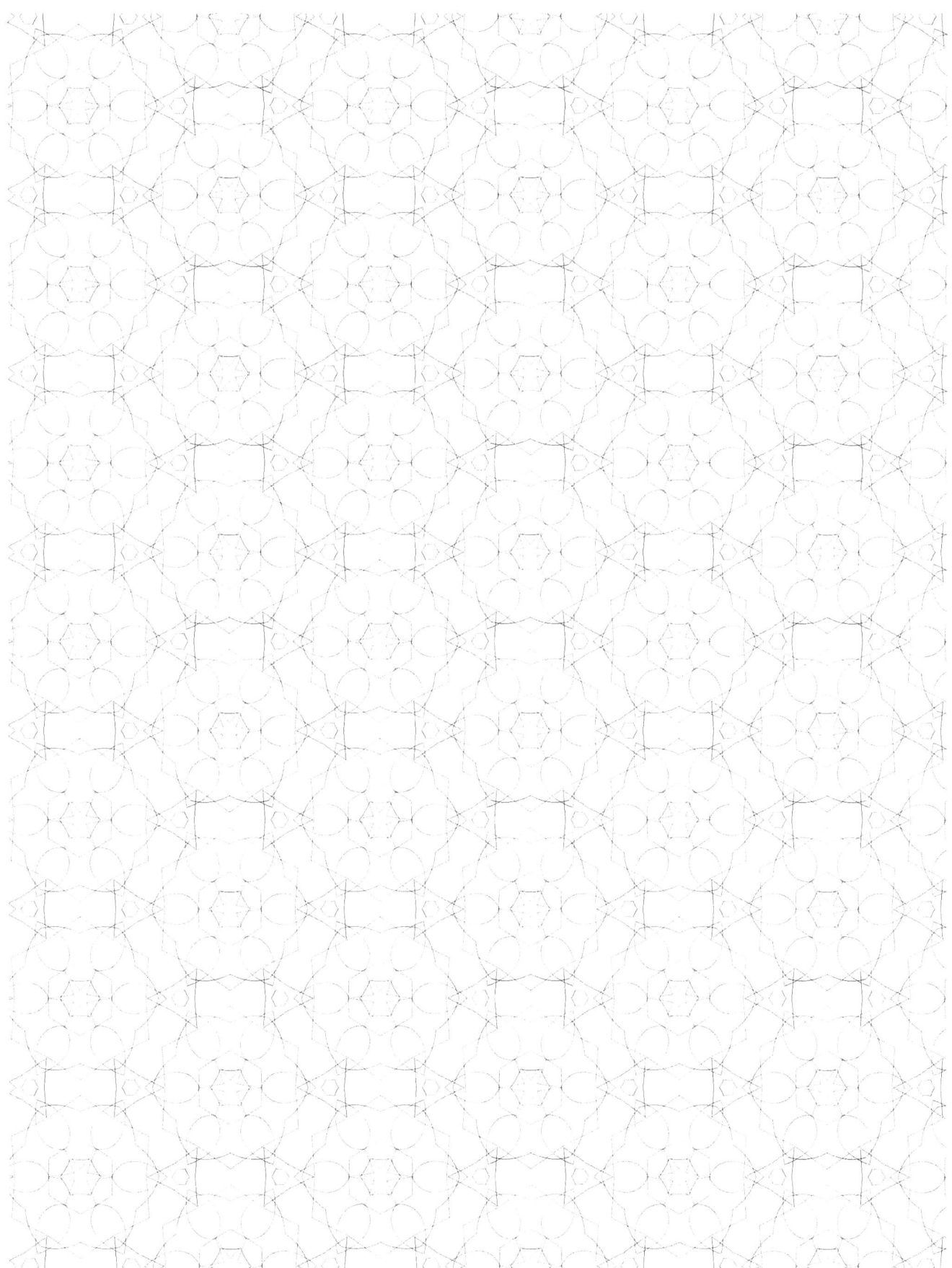

42

48

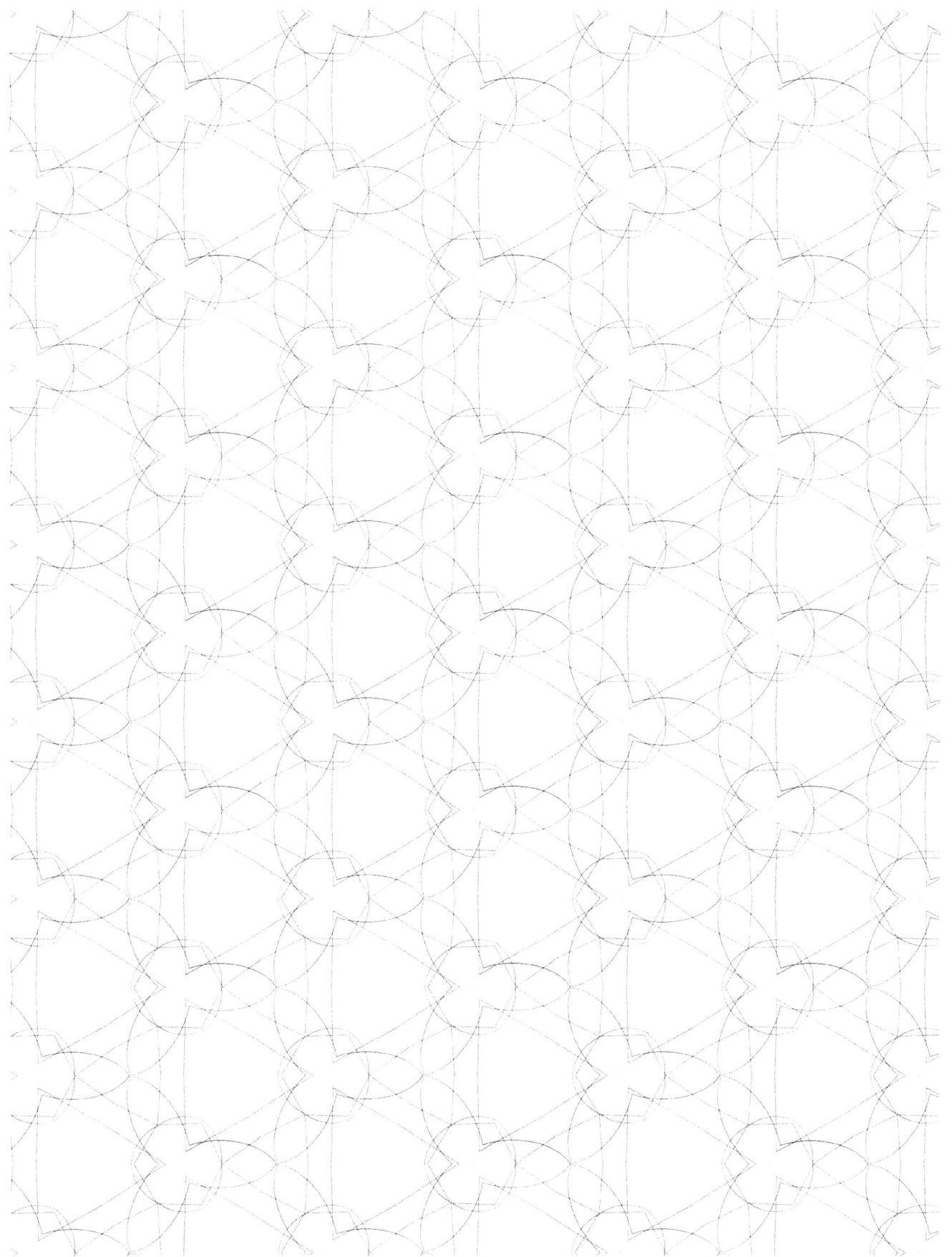

61

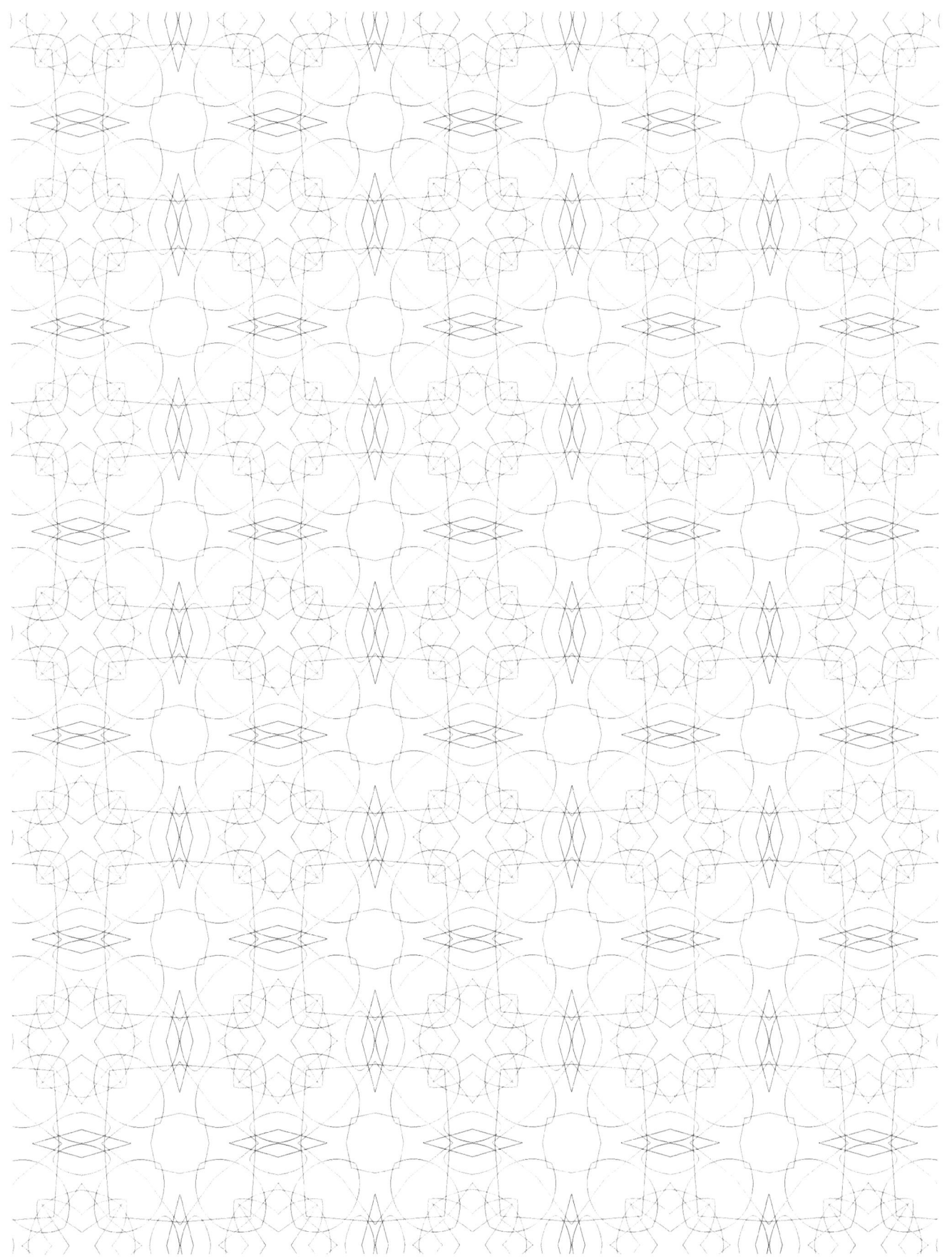

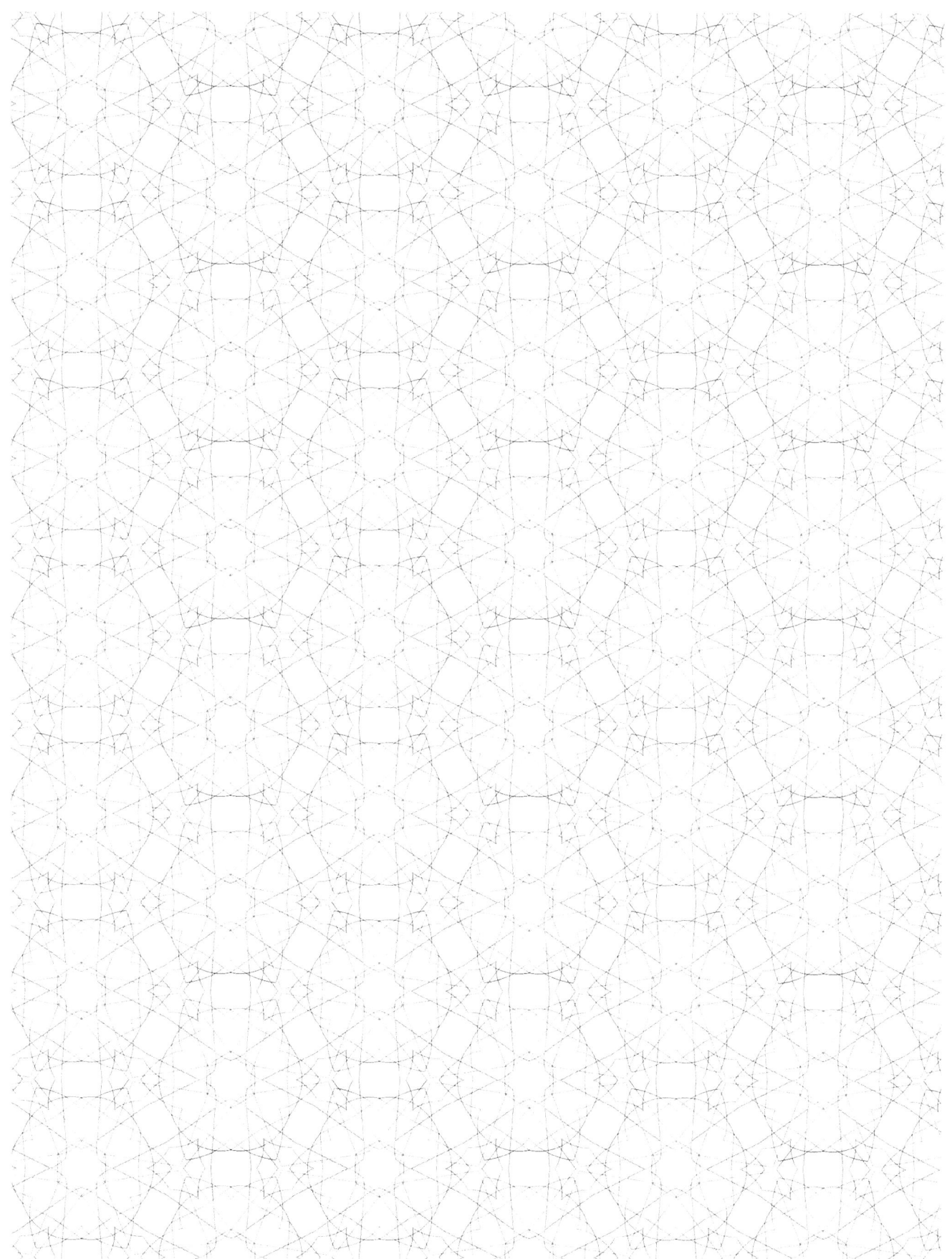

77

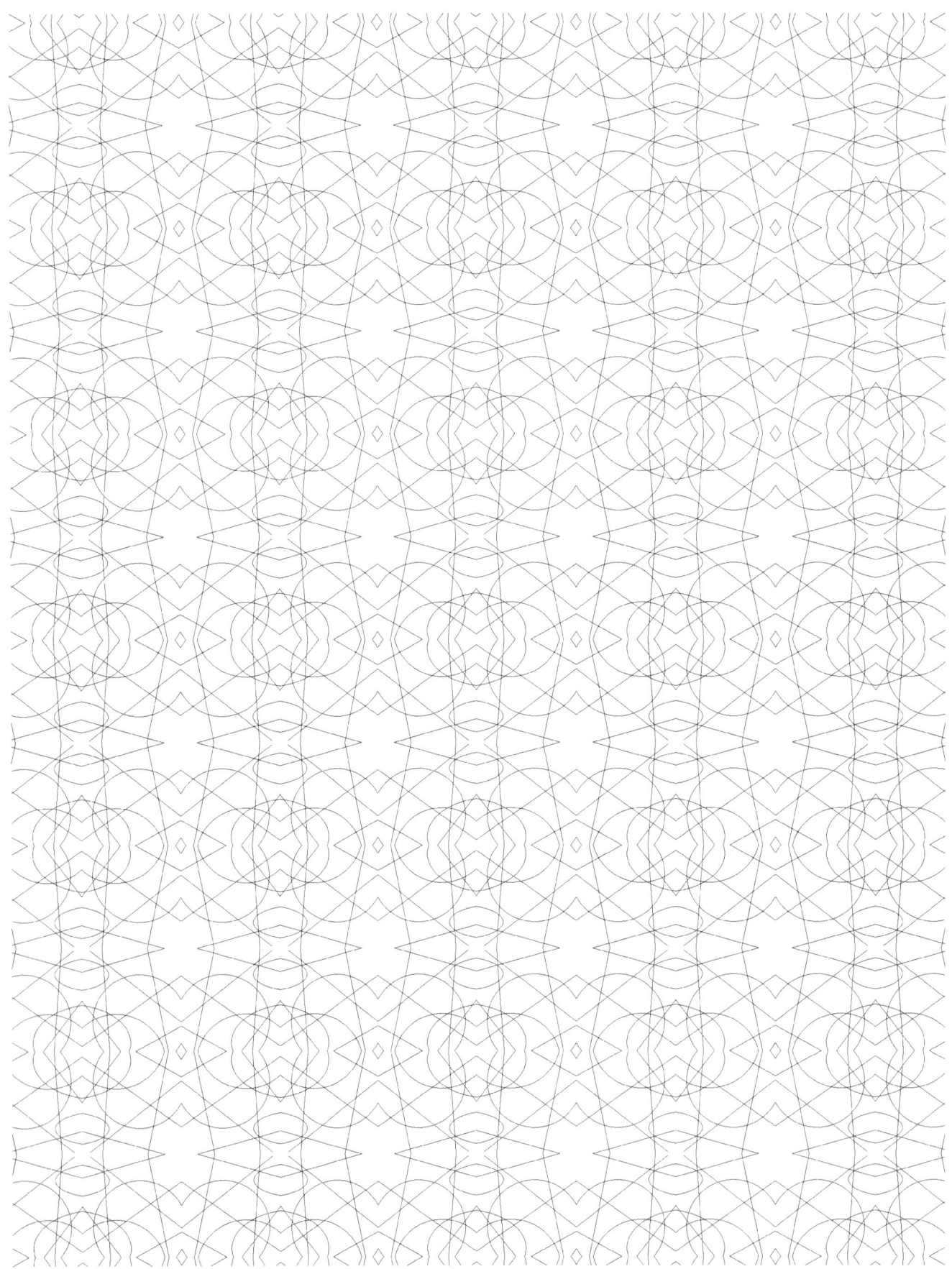

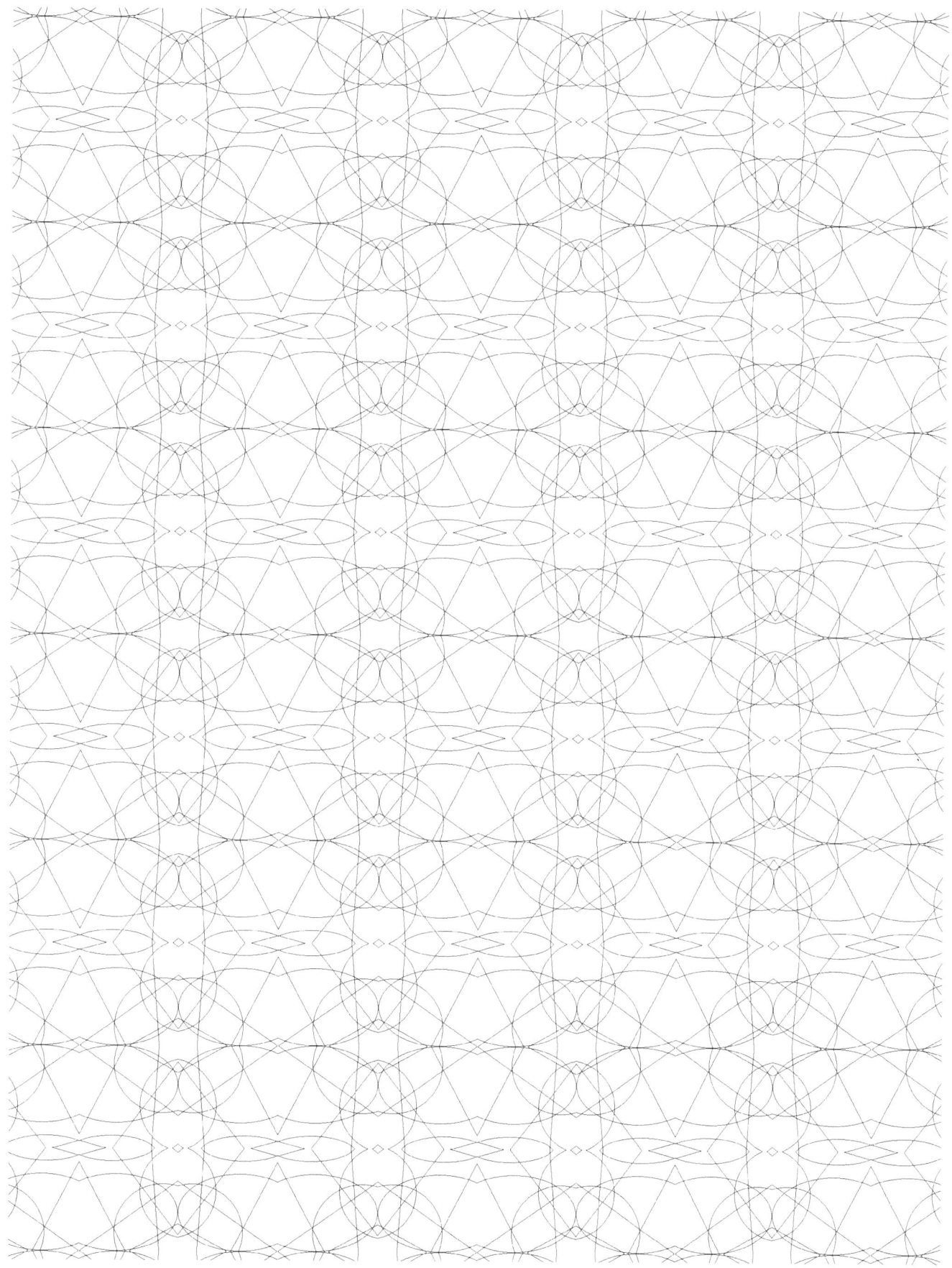

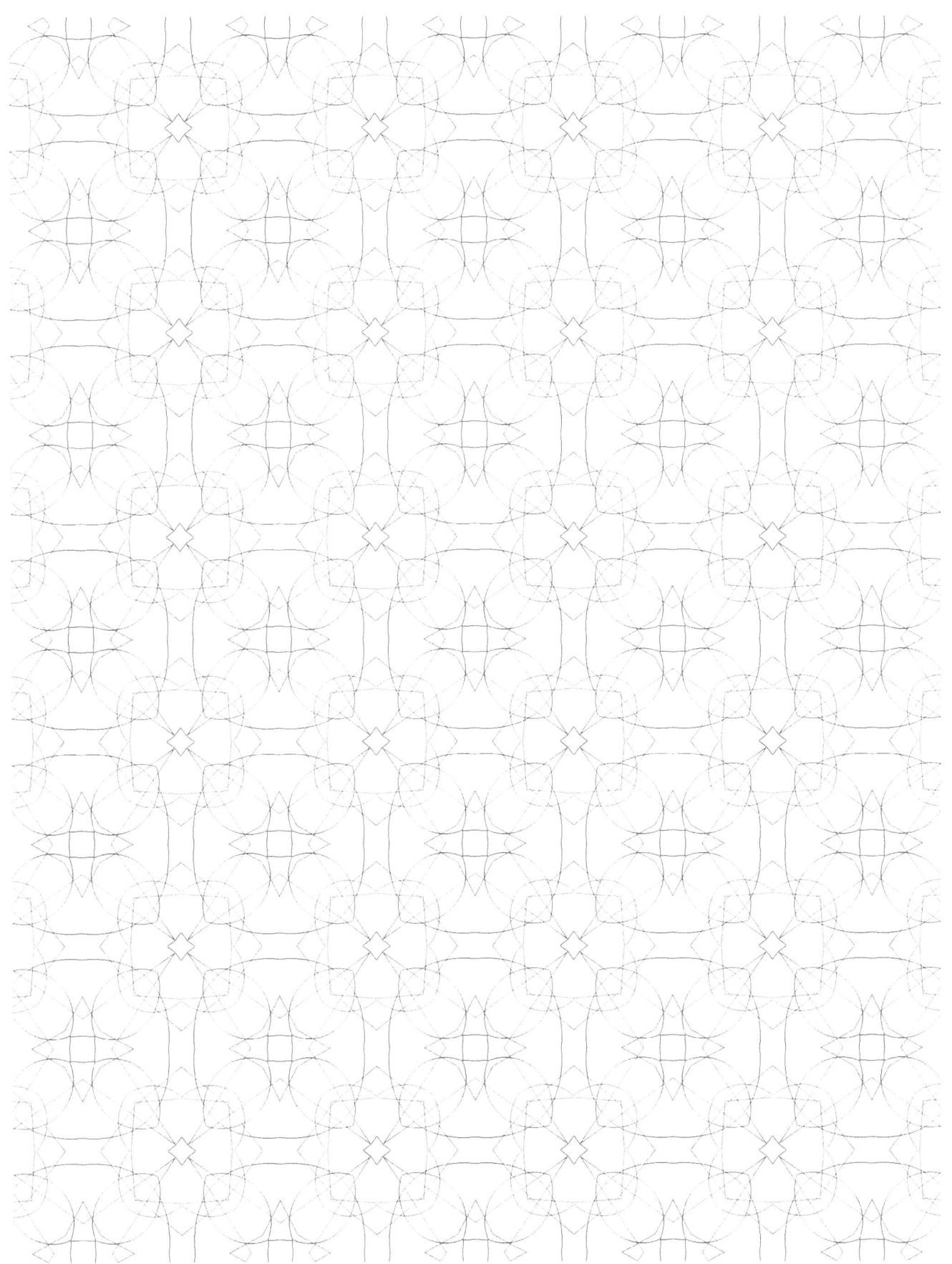

85

88

98

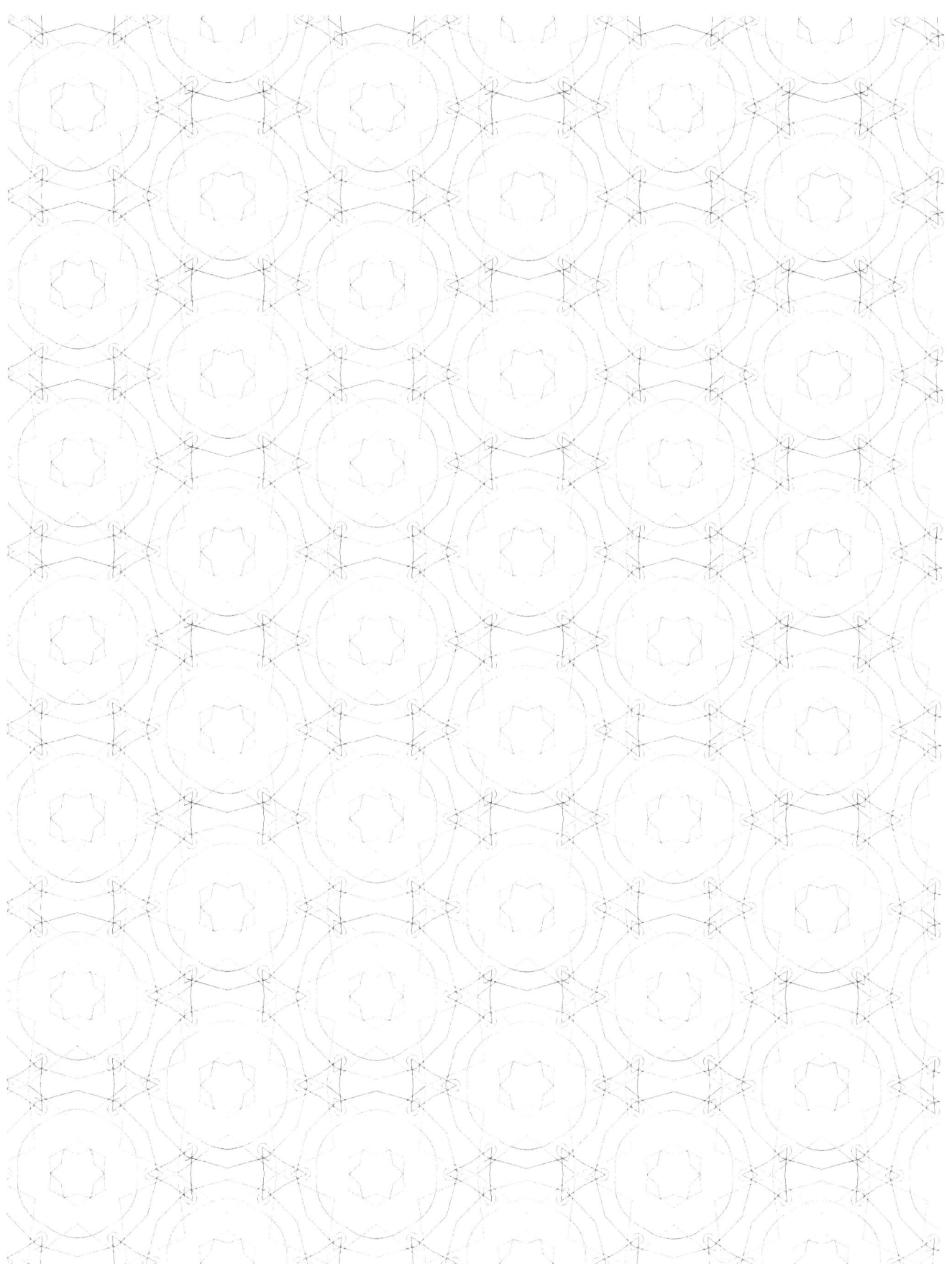

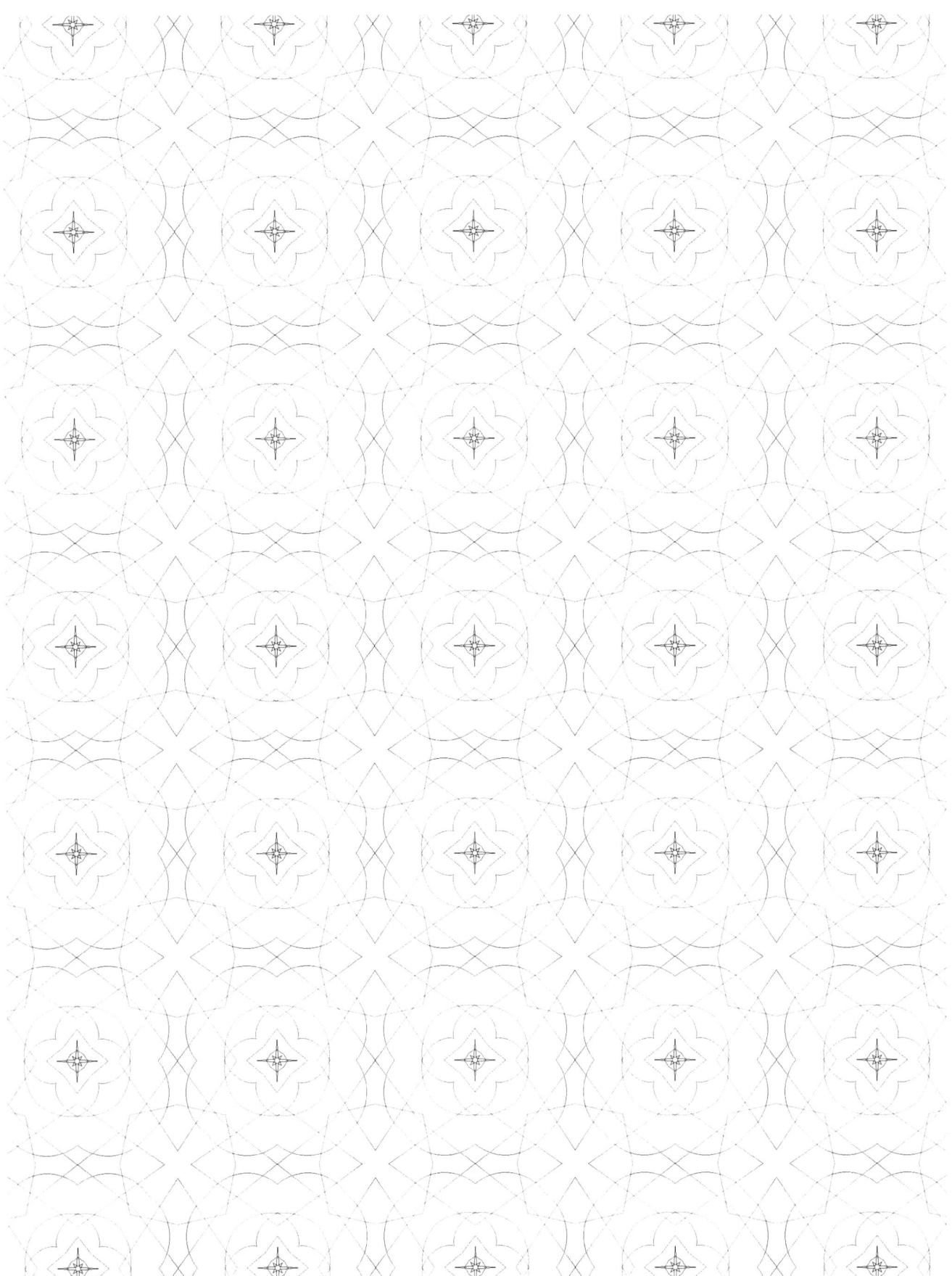

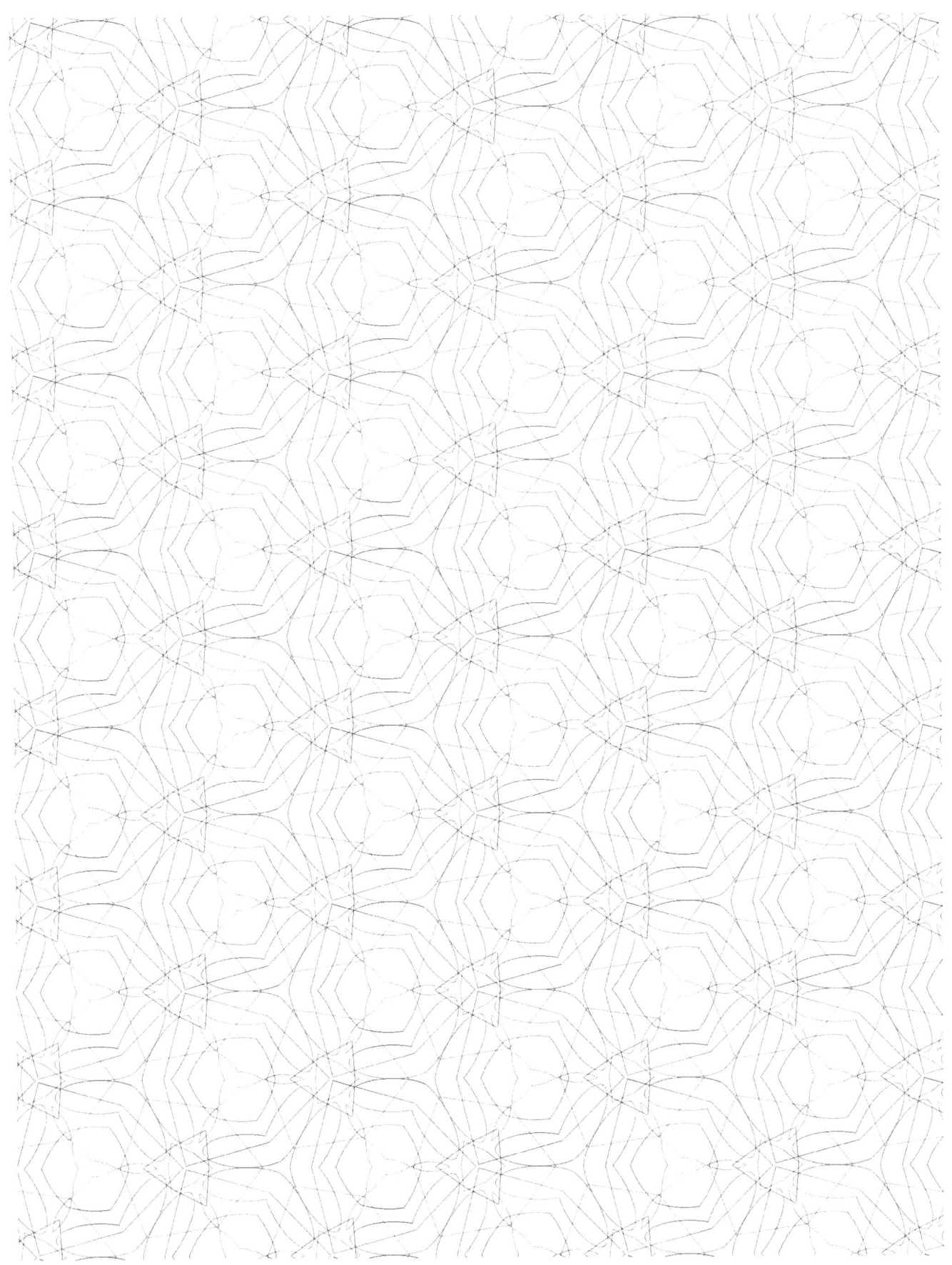

115

116

118

119

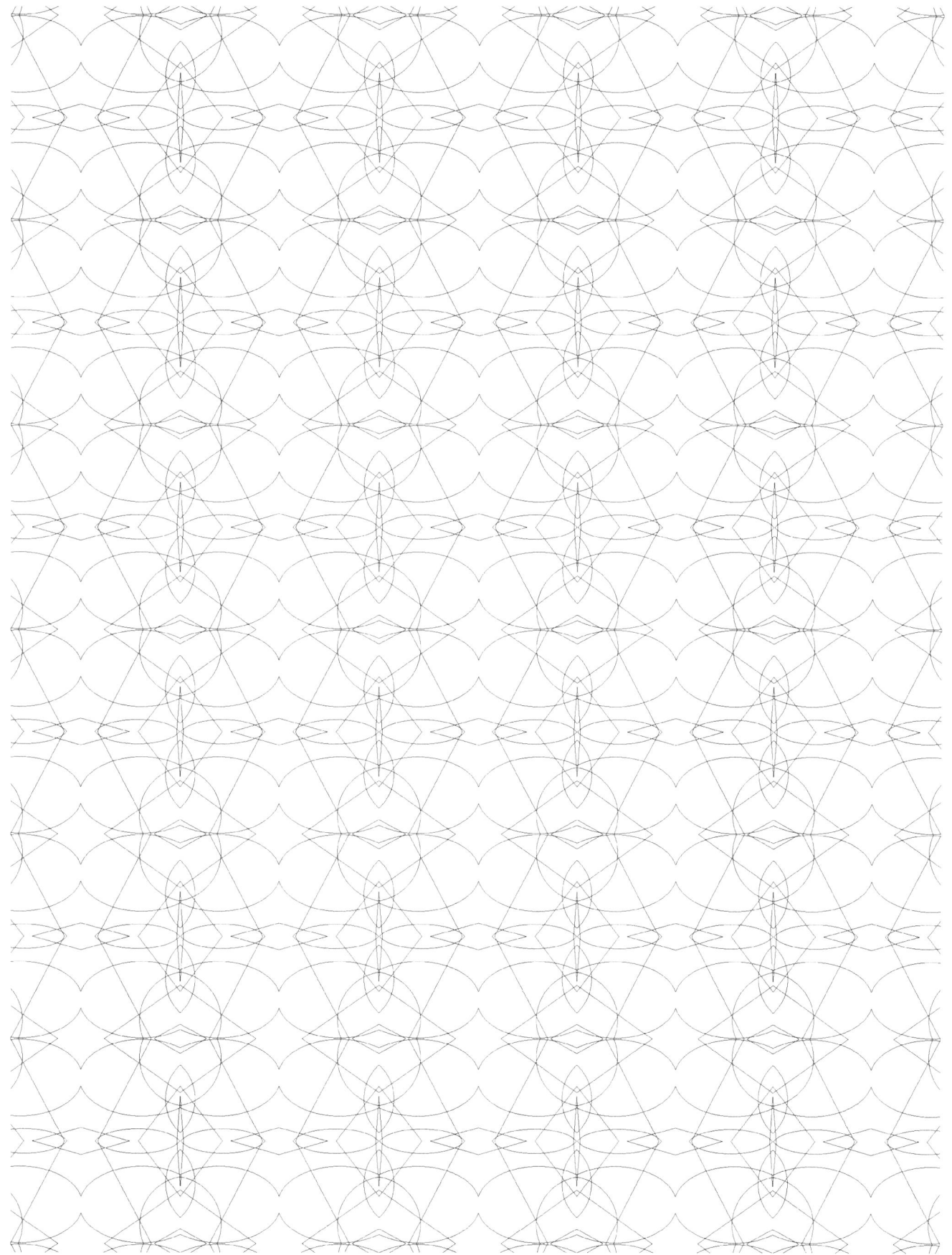

126

128

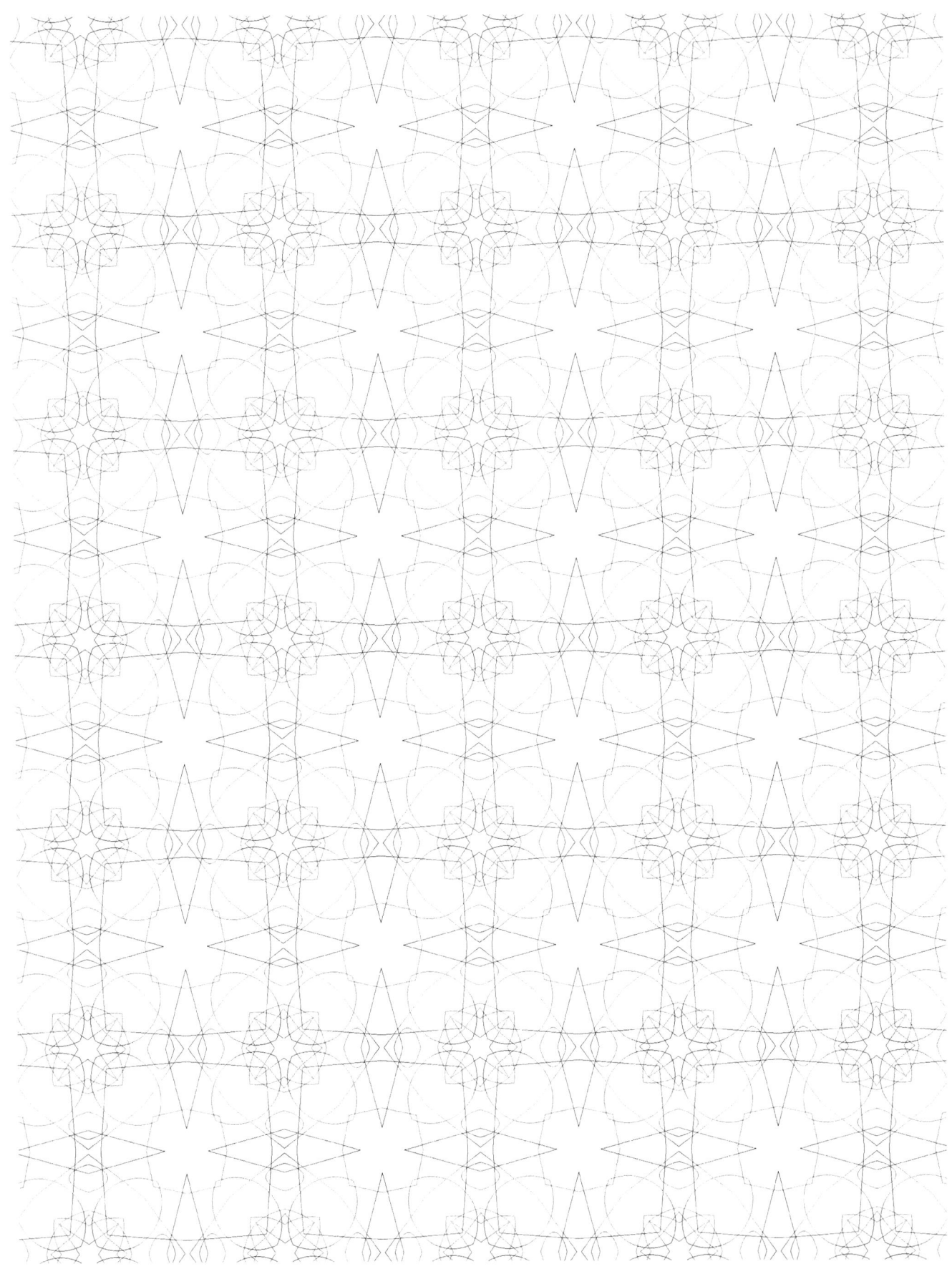

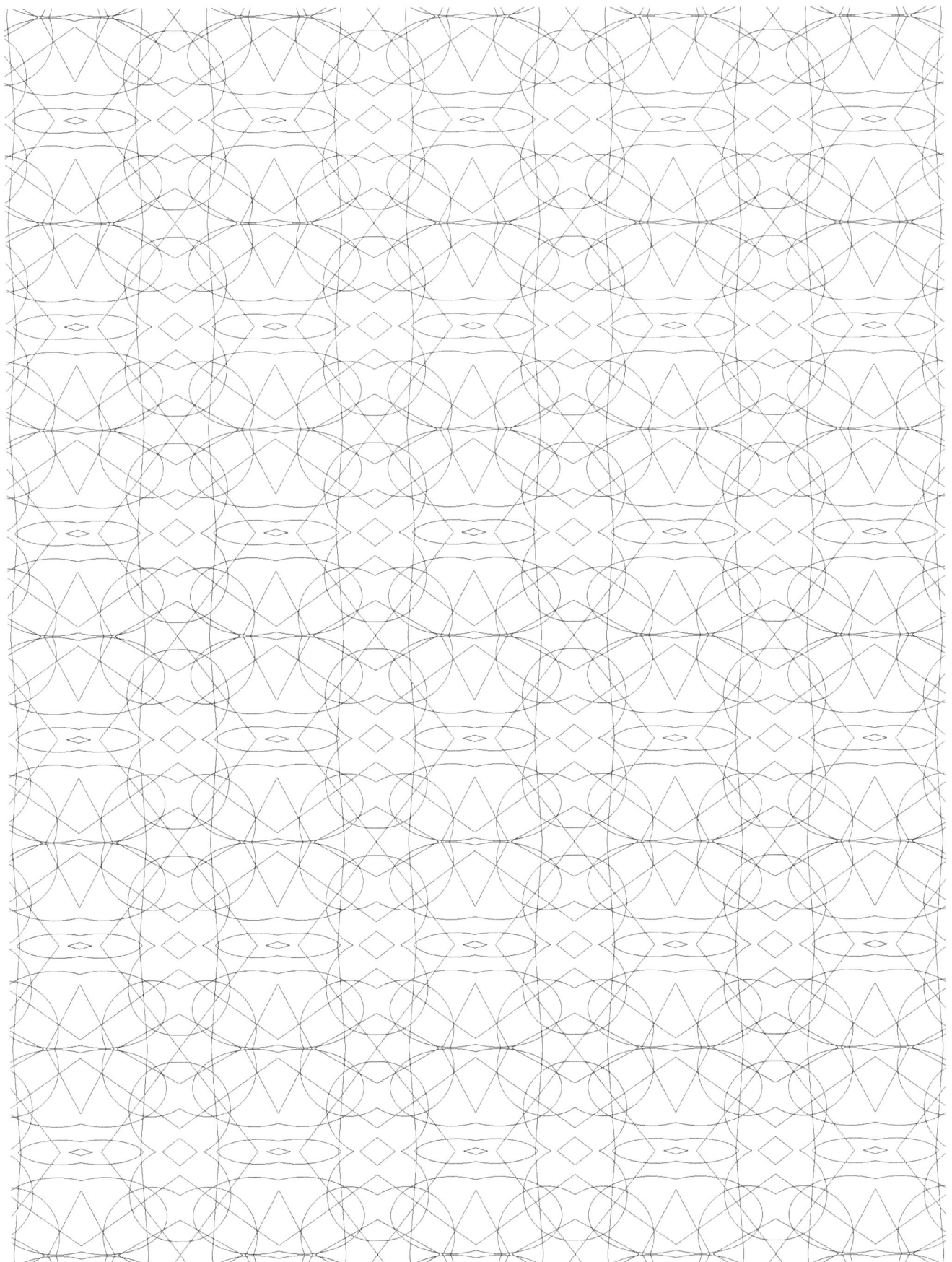

134

138

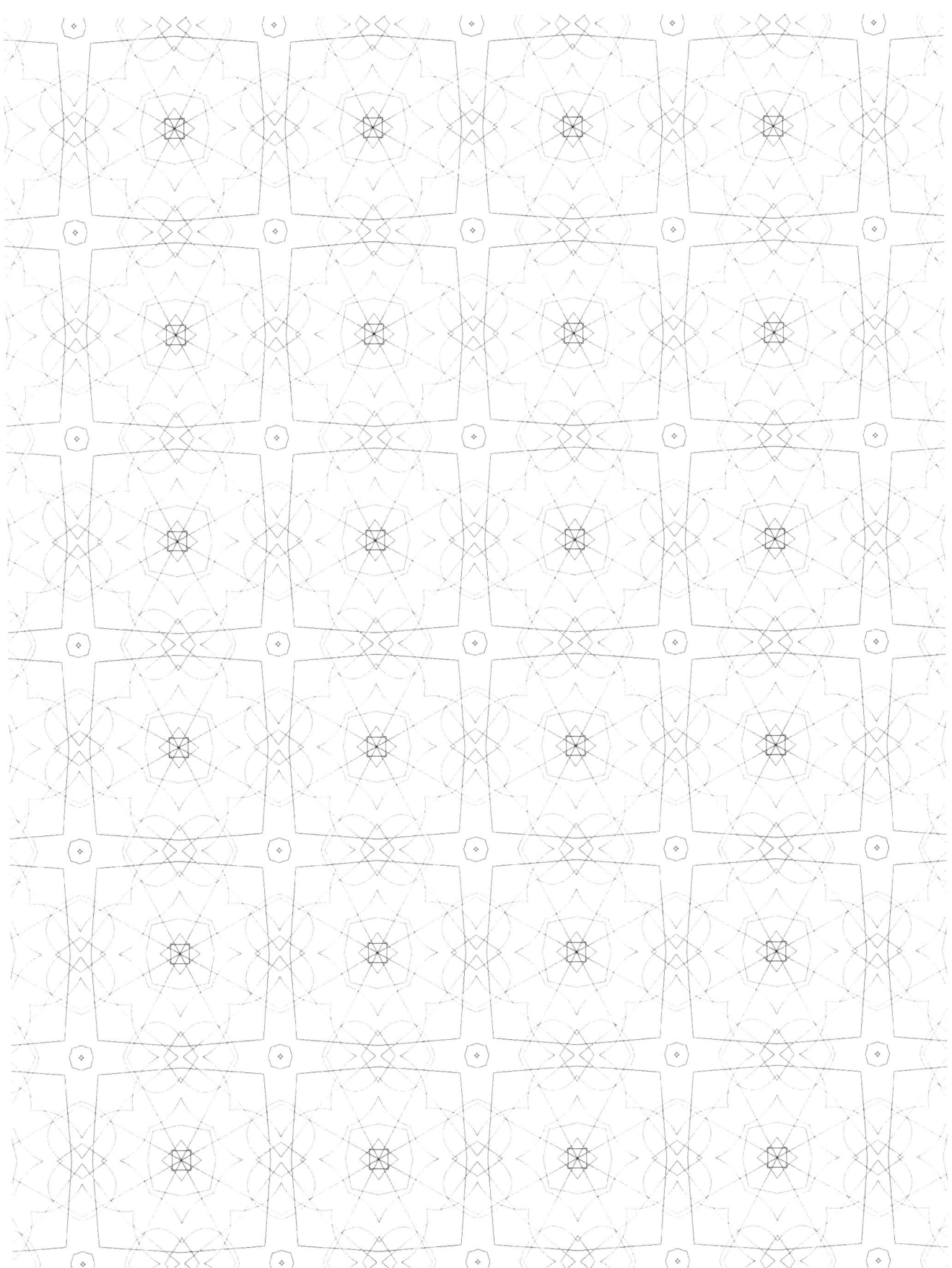

145

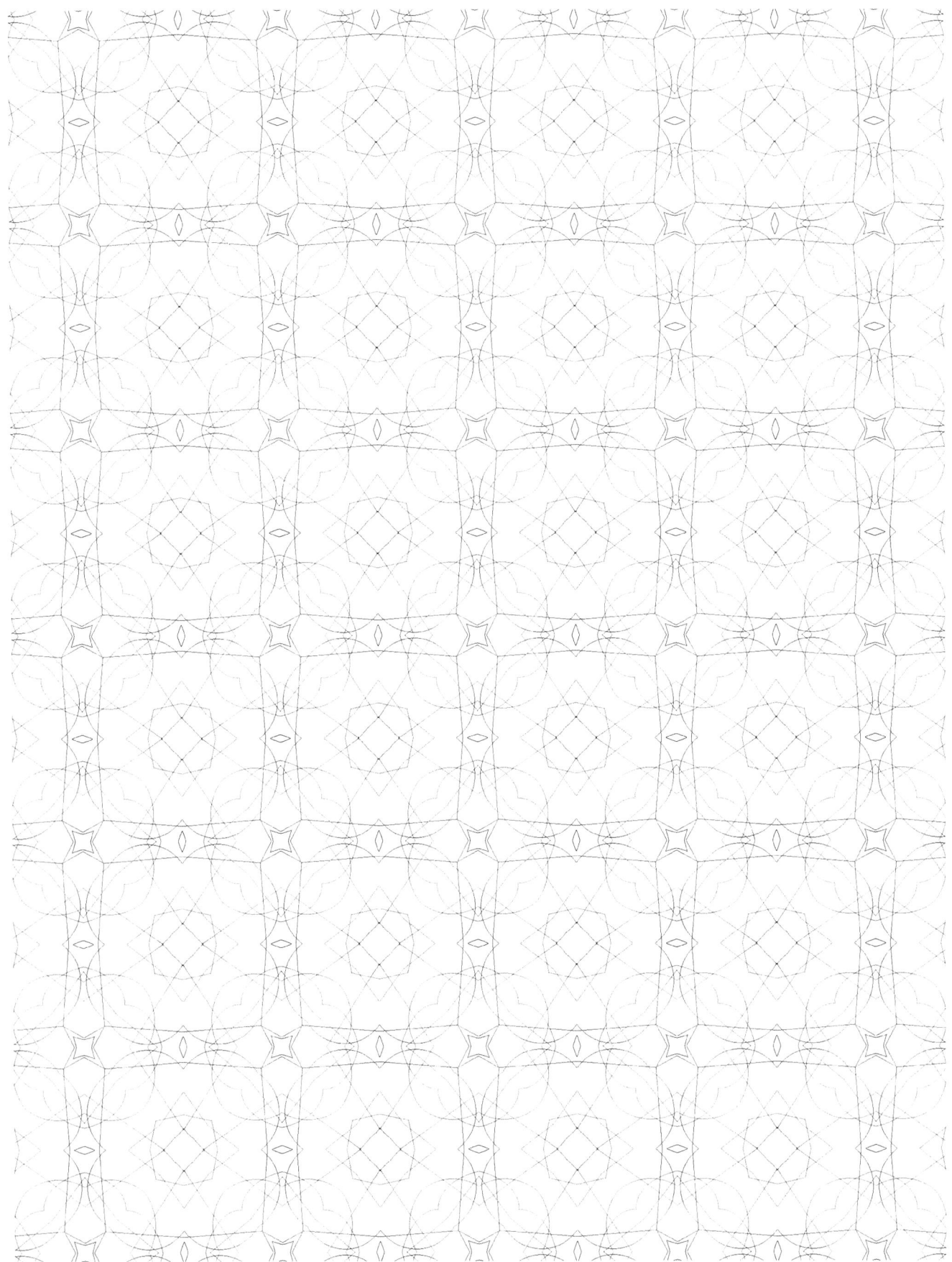

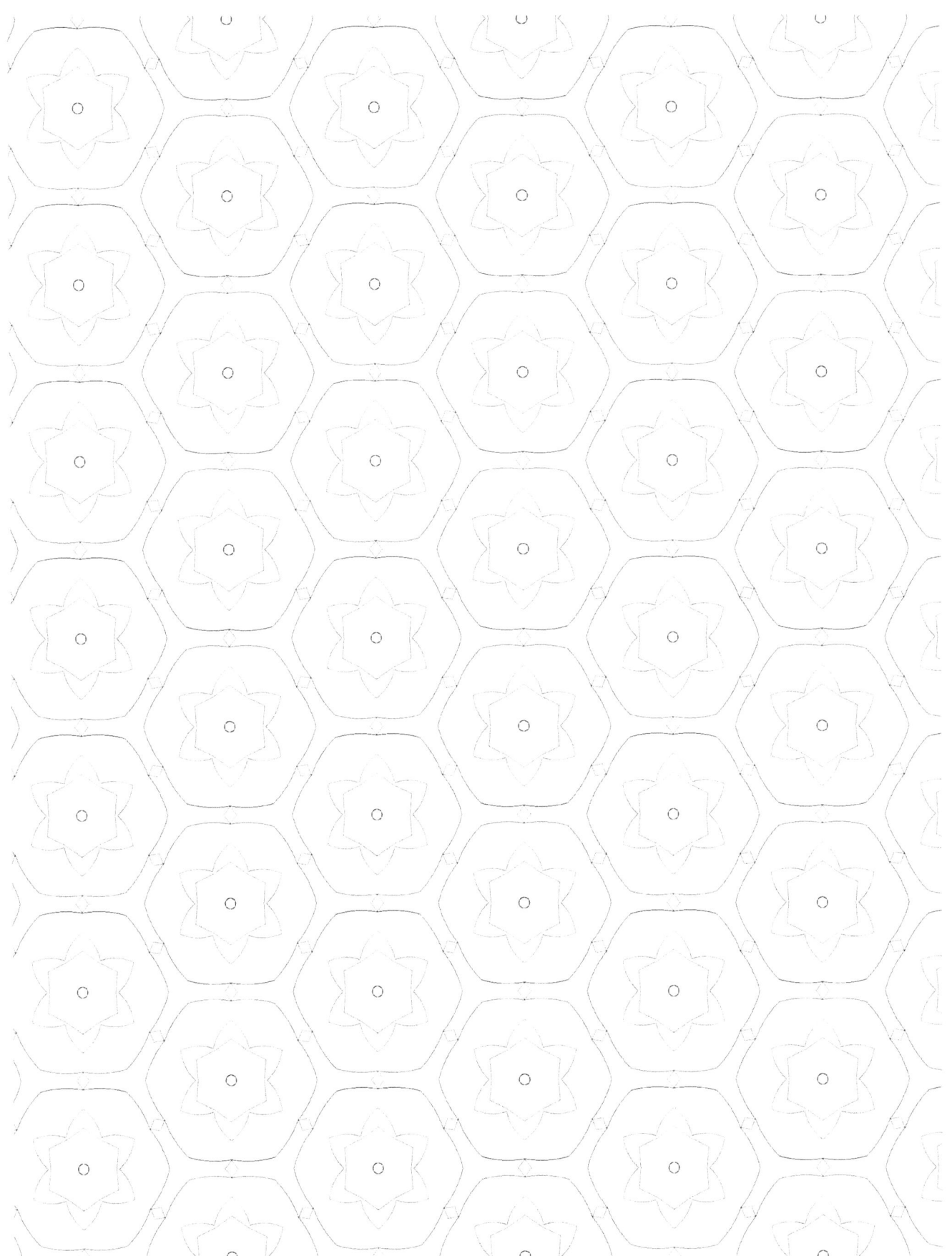

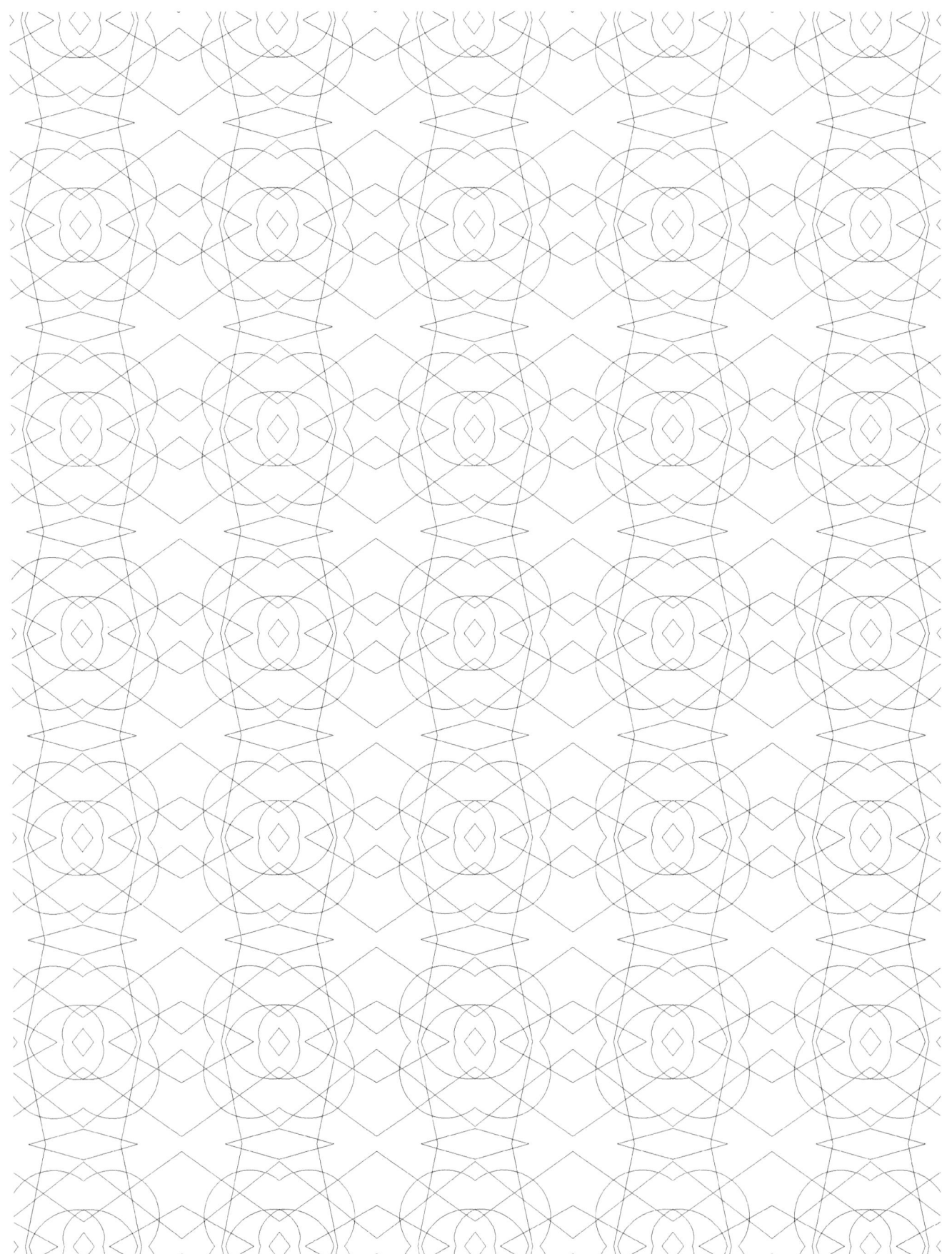

155

157

159

www.ingramcontent.com/pod-product-compliance
Lightning Source LLC
Chambersburg PA
CBHW081149180526
45170CB00006B/1993